Cornerstones of Freedom

Mount Rushmore

ANDREW SANTELLA

CHILDREN'S PRESS®
A Division of Grolier Publishing
New York • London • Hong Kong • Sydney
Danbury, Connecticut

Visit Children's Press on the Internet at:
http://publishing.grolier.com

Library of Congress Cataloging-in-Publication Data

Santella, Andrew.
    Mount Rushmore / Andrew Santella.
        p. cm.—(Cornerstones of freedom)
    Includes index.
    Summary: Relates how the Mount Rushmore National Memorial, known
as "The Shrine of Democracy," was conceived, designed, and created.
    ISBN: 0-516-21140-4 (lib. bdg.)   0-516-26459-1 (pbk.)
        1. Mount Rushmore National Memorial (S.D.)—Juvenile literature.
    [1. Mount Rushmore National Memorial (S.D.) 2. National monuments.]
    I. Title. II. Series.
    F657.R8S26   1999
    978.3'93—dc21
                                                    98-3494
                                                      CIP
                                                       AC

GROLIER
PUBLISHING

The Mount Rushmore National Memorial honors four of the greatest United States presidents. It is also a monument to the vision of one dedicated artist.

Mount Rushmore National Memorial is one of South Dakota's most-visited sites.

Gutzon Borglum

The memorial is one of the world's most spectacular pieces of sculpture. It has been called "The Shrine of Democracy." The huge likenesses of George Washington, Thomas Jefferson, Abraham Lincoln, and Theodore Roosevelt are carved into the granite wall of Mount Rushmore. The work was designed by the American sculptor Gutzon Borglum. Over fourteen years, he and his son directed the painstaking labor that went into creating the memorial. Against daunting odds, Borglum and his team created an awe-inspiring monument that will endure through the ages.

Borglum and his team blasted 8 million pounds (4 million kilograms) of stone off the mountainside to complete the sculpture. Each of the four faces carved into the mountain is 60 feet (18 meters) long. Borglum's artistry combined with the rugged natural beauty of the Black Hills of South Dakota to create a stunning scene. The memorial is one of the most recognizable sites in the world.

The memorial's story begins in the early 1920s when a South Dakota historian named Doane Robinson first suggested that a huge monument be built in the Black Hills. Robinson knew that South Dakota's Black Hills region was one of the most scenic in the country. He wanted others to know it, too. What the area needed, he believed, was a special attraction to draw visitors.

At around the same time, Gutzon Borglum was in Georgia, working on just the kind of project that Robinson had in mind. Borglum was chiseling the gigantic images of Southern heroes of the Civil War into a Georgia mountainside. Robinson heard about Borglum's Georgia project and wondered if something similar could be done in South Dakota. He knew that this was the kind of project that would attract the nation's attention. And, if it was ever completed, it would be sure to attract visitors.

In 1924, he wrote a letter to Gutzon Borglum. Robinson invited him to visit the Black Hills, look over the area, and decide if he could create a huge work of art there.

The natural beauty of the Black Hills region inspired Doane Robinson to draw visitors to the area.

Robinson could not have made a better choice. Borglum's parents had come to the United States from Denmark. Borglum himself was born in Idaho in 1867. He grew up in Nebraska, but left to study in California when he was seventeen years old. He studied painting in San Francisco and then in Paris, France. Soon, he devoted himself exclusively to sculpture. He moved to England, where his reputation grew. His work made him an internationally known artist. But it was Borglum's work in the United States that made Robinson contact him.

In 1901, one of Borglum's works became the first piece of American sculpture purchased by the Metropolitan Museum of Art in New York. In 1909, Borglum sculpted a bust of Abraham Lincoln that is now in the Capitol Rotunda in Washington, D.C. It was a huge sculpture, carved from a 6-ton block of marble. That led to work on an even grander scale. By 1915, Borglum began working on his enormous memorial carved into the side of Stone Mountain in Georgia. Borglum never finished that project. A dispute with his patrons caused him to resign. But Doane Robinson took note that Borglum was an artist who was willing to take on the challenge of sculpting the side of a mountain.

Ancient Egyptians and Mesopotamians had made similar works thousands of years earlier. They cut enormous statues out of natural rock formations. Borglum wanted to create works of art that were just as massive and impressive. He believed that colossal art was "soul-stirring."

Borglum was known as an artist who thought big. His plans for the Stone Mountain memorial were ambitious. In fact, Borglum was so committed to his vision that many found him difficult to work with. His uncompromising attitude led to problems on the Stone Mountain job. When he didn't get to finish the project, he was bitterly disappointed. He also became more determined than ever to complete a mammoth memorial. If he couldn't do it at Stone Mountain, he would do it elsewhere.

Georgia's Stone Mountain is a memorial to Southern leaders of the Civil War (from left): Jefferson Davis, Robert E. Lee, and Stonewall Jackson.

As Borglum's fame spread, he received more and more offers to do large sculptures. He considered many opportunities, but only one seemed right to him. Something attracted Borglum to the Black Hills of South Dakota. Maybe it was Borglum's background as the son of western pioneers. All his life, Borglum promoted the virtues of his native land. When the chance came to do a massive work of art in the American West, he could hardly pass it up.

His first visit to the Black Hills made him even more enthusiastic. In September 1924, Borglum came to South Dakota to meet with Robinson. At that time, Robinson didn't have in mind a monument to presidents. He was thinking of honoring great figures from the American West. He had proposed the explorers Meriwether Lewis and William Clark or the Oglala Sioux leader Red Cloud. Lewis and Clark gained fame for their 1804–06 expedition of the Louisiana Purchase, from St. Louis, Missouri, to present-day Astoria, Oregon, and back. Red Cloud was an American-Indian warrior and chief. During the 1860s, Red Cloud led raids on U.S. Army forts in Wyoming and Montana that had been built in Sioux territory. In 1868, the army abandoned the forts.

Red Cloud declared war on the U.S. government for building forts in Sioux territory.

As a result, Red Cloud is known as the only American Indian who ever won a war against the U.S. government.

Later it was decided to build a memorial to great presidents. Robinson didn't have Mount Rushmore itself in mind as the site for the monument. He considered several other places in the Black Hills for the project. One of those areas was the Needles, a series of jagged, rugged peaks. It was the first place Robinson and Borglum visited. The two men rode horses for miles over the rugged terrain. Borglum was amazed at the beauty of the jagged peaks. The views were stunning. Rock formations jutted skyward. Deep canyons split the pine forests. Trout flourished in clear streams and wildlife teemed in the woods. "Here is the place," Borglum said to Robinson. "American history shall march along that skyline."

Robinson and Borglum first considered the Needles region of South Dakota as the place to establish a monument.

As it turned out, the irregular peaks of the Needles were too badly weathered to stand up to carving. But that didn't discourage Borglum. Later on the trip, he told a South Dakota audience, "I know of no grouping of rock formations that equals those found in the Black Hills . . . nor any that is so suitable to sculpture." Finishing with a flourish, he called the hills a "garden of the gods." Borglum was still thinking big. He wanted the residents of the area to think big right along with him.

It wasn't until the next year (1925), though, that Borglum settled on the site for his work. It was an enormous mountain. Its main wall was almost 500 feet (152 m) long, large enough for the work he had in mind. It towered over the other nearby peaks, making it visible from a

Mount Rushmore in 1925, before the project began

distance. The granite sides of the mountain were stable enough to stand up to carving. The walls loomed above slopes of wildflowers and timber. Best of all, the mountain faced southeast, giving it exposure to sunlight. It was known to locals as Mount Rushmore. On its surface, Borglum would etch his grand vision.

One day in August 1925, Borglum and his son Lincoln set out with a small group to climb Mount Rushmore. It was their first trip up the mountain that would be the center of their lives for years to come. It was a grueling climb. In some places, the group had to scale walls that went straight up. But everyone in the group made it to the top of the cliff—even the 58-year-old sculptor and his 13-year-old son.

Gutzon Borglum (second from right) and the members of his party prepare to leave the town of Keystone, South Dakota, for their first climb up Mount Rushmore. (Lincoln Borglum is standing next to his father.)

George Washington

Thomas Jefferson

Abraham Lincoln

Theodore Roosevelt

Difficult as it was, the climb was well worth it. The views from the top were stunning. Borglum and the others could see mile after mile of mountains and plains stretching into the distance—west into Wyoming, east to the plains of South Dakota. Later Borglum wrote that he felt like he was in another world. It was then that he decided that "plans must change. The vastness I saw here demanded it." Once again, Borglum's plans were getting bigger, his vision grander.

Borglum decided that he couldn't limit himself to a monument to heroes of the Old West. Instead, he decided the site called for a "great American memorial"—one that honored the giants of American history. Before long, the sculptor was drawing sketches of George Washington and Abraham Lincoln. Soon he was including Thomas Jefferson, as well. And as he realized how much room he had to work with on the massive mountain, Borglum grew even bolder. "Here we have such stone large enough for not one but three or four or five figures," he wrote.

Borglum wanted the memorial to tell the story of the United States. His idea was to pay tribute to the presidents who saw the nation through its founding, its growth, its preservation and its development. In a speech in Rapid City, he declared that the figures carved into the mountain were "to be those of George

Washington, Thomas Jefferson, Abraham Lincoln, and Theodore Roosevelt."

Washington served as the first president of the United States, from 1789 to 1797. Jefferson doubled the size of the United States with the Louisiana Purchase and was the country's third president, from 1801 to 1809. Lincoln, who insured the preservation of the Union during the Civil War, served as the sixteenth president, from 1861 to 1865. And Roosevelt, representing the United States's development as a powerful nation, was the twenty-sixth president, from 1901 to 1909.

Borglum worked in his studio at the base of Mount Rushmore to turn his sketches into plaster models before they were actually carved into the mountain.

Although Borglum's masterpiece was already taking shape in his mind, he still wasn't sure it could really be done. He had taken great care in choosing Mount Rushmore for his work. But until he began sculpting, he couldn't know if the mountain held some flaw that would ruin his work. It was weather-beaten and aged. It had stood in the heart of the Black Hills for millions of years. It showed its age.

Long before Borglum carved it, wind and rain had already etched its face. Mount Rushmore's cliff wall has been described as looking like elephant skin—gray and wrinkled. It was lined

A close-up view of Mount Rushmore's surface

with crevices. Borglum had to take these crevices into consideration in designing his monument. But at least he could see them. Until he began carving, he had no way of knowing the condition of the stone inside the cliff. Would it be too hard to cut? Would it be too brittle? Would there be flaws in the stone that would mar his monument?

Borglum could not answer any of these questions until he began cutting into the face of Mount Rushmore. Still, he did not let doubts delay him. He forged ahead, certain that Rushmore was the right place for the memorial. But first he had to convince others that Mount Rushmore was the wise choice. Senator Peter Norbeck of South Dakota had been involved in the project since its earliest stages. He was willing to take Borglum's word that Rushmore offered the best sculpting surface. But what about other considerations? For one thing, the remote cliff was far from good roads. And roads would certainly be needed to move workers and haul equipment to and from the site.

Senator Peter Norbeck

Borglum did not let the senator's objections slow him. He was itching to begin work on the mountain. He even announced that he planned to dedicate the site in October 1925. That was news to Senator Norbeck. "This man works so fast," wrote the senator, "that it is hard . . . even to keep track of him."

There was one detail that still needed to be worked out, however. Who was going to pay for the work on Mount Rushmore? Borglum had already promised the people of South Dakota that they would not pay the bill for the memorial. But he never said exactly how it would be paid for. A group of Rapid City merchants bailed Borglum out temporarily when they began a fundraising drive to cover some of the initial fees. Much more money would be needed, though.

One thing that was not lacking at this point was the support of the area population. As Dedication Day (October 1, 1925) neared, excitement about the memorial grew. Locals pitched in to make sure the dedication went off smoothly. A women's group stitched five huge American flags, 18 feet (5 m) wide by 30 feet (9 m) long. Men from the town of Keystone used their own axes and shovels to clear a road to Mount Rushmore. And on the big day itself, some three thousand people gathered to see Borglum and Senator Norbeck dedicate the memorial. The sculptor promised that work on the image of George Washington would be done within a year. "Meet me here a year from today and we will dedicate it," he told the cheering crowd.

Borglum didn't meet that deadline. He didn't even come close. But he and his supporters

slowly made progress. A local fund-raising drive netted its goal of $25,000. The national and state legislation needed for the completion of the project was passed. The state built a road to Mount Rushmore. And, in 1927, the Black Hills received a famous visitor. President Calvin Coolidge came to vacation near Mount Rushmore for three months. Borglum did not pass up the chance for publicity that the president's visit offered. On August 10, 1927, he dedicated Mount Rushmore again.

Part of the crowd at the first dedication, which was held on October 1, 1925

The second dedication was a lot like the first. There were speeches and a flag-raising ceremony. But this time, the president of the United States was there. His presence gave even greater importance to the event. Coolidge wore cowboy boots and a western hat and he listened to Borglum talk about his project. The sculptor called it "a memorial to the first modern republic in the western world." Then Borglum was lowered in a harness and drilled the first holes in the side of the mountain. Now the task of actually building the memorial was at long last about to begin.

Borglum's crew operated from a

Above: President Calvin Coolidge, speaking at the second dedication of Mount Rushmore

Right: Workers stand atop Mount Rushmore. The lines on the mountainside indicate places Borglum has marked off to begin carving.

base called Doane Mountain, named for Doane Robinson, located across a gulch from Mount Rushmore. By fall, the base was a cluster of buildings including a blacksmith shop, a bunkhouse, a restaurant, and a studio for the sculptor. The base was connected to Mount Rushmore by a cable that supported a large steel bucket loaded with supplies. The cable-way was not safe enough for the crew, though. Instead, they had to walk up hundreds of stairs every day to get to their work stations. It was the equivalent of walking up a forty-story building.

The restaurant building at the workers' base camp

19

The workers' first task was to measure a rough outline for the head of George Washington. Then they could begin peeling away the stone to get to the clean surface that would be sculpted. Borglum's crew did their work suspended from the top of the mountain in swings. Dangling in mid-air, they used jackhammers to drill holes in the side of the mountain and chip away at it. This took so long that soon Borglum was ready to try another solution. In late October, they began blasting away rock with dynamite. Eventually about 500,000 tons of stone was blasted off the mountain. The figure of Washington was the first to be completed. It was not ready for unveiling until 1930.

Workers lower themselves onto the rock's surface to begin work on the head of George Washington.

But an even larger problem was looming. Funds for the project were running low. In 1928, no work at all was done on the monument. It took the support of the federal government to get work on Mount Rushmore started again. Senator Norbeck and South Dakota Congressman William Williamson introduced legislation to provide federal funding. Their bill called for the government to pay for half the cost of the memorial, up to $250,000. The funding would not be direct, though. It would come in the form of "matching funds." That is, the government would contribute one dollar for every dollar raised from private sources. It was signed into law by President Coolidge on February 25, 1929.

In July 1929, the Mount Rushmore National Memorial Commission visited the site to check on the work's progress. (In the front row are pictured Doane Robinson, second from left, and Gutzon Borglum, fourth from left.)

In this photograph, taken several years into the project, Borglum travels on the cableway from the camp to the mountain to direct the carving.

The law's passage meant that work on Mount Rushmore could resume. But it didn't solve all the financial problems. In 1929, not long after the Mount Rushmore law was passed, the stock market crashed and the nation fell into the Great Depression. Banks closed, ordinary people lost their jobs, and the entire national economy was in peril. Under such circumstances, private funds for the monument were scarce. And if little money could be raised from private sources, just as little would come from the government.

Over the next few years, financial problems would plague the Mount Rushmore operation. A regular supply of money was needed to pay workers and to keep equipment running. Every so often, money would run low and work would have to stop. Then a new source of funds would be discovered and work would start up again—

until the next crisis. The situation made the project a very lengthy one. It wasn't until 1934 that the problem was solved. That year, the Mount Rushmore legislation was changed to provide for direct appropriation. That meant there was a steady supply of money flowing to keep the work going.

But even with financial problems solved, the weather could still cause trouble. When temperatures dipped down around 0 degrees Fahrenheit (18 degrees Celsius), or when rain or snow was severe, work stopped. Eventually Borglum had temporary shelters set up on the sides of the mountains to protect his workers from the elements.

Shelters on the mountain protected workers from the harsh effects of the weather.

Most of the workers on the mountain were local men. Some had been miners or ranchers or lumbermen. Many were struggling to make ends meet during the Depression. At Mount Rushmore, they found work they could believe in. The hours were long and the work was hard. But most were proud to be working on a project of such importance. Depending on how much money was available, as many as seventy workers might be toiling on the mountain at once. In leaner times, there might be only a handful at work.

They started work at 7:30 A.M. with a long climb to the top of Mount Rushmore. Workmen were lowered to their assigned stations to drill holes in the surface of the mountain. Then they filled the holes with explosive powder. They ignited the powder twice a day—at lunchtime and at the end of the day. The blasts echoed through the hills and canyons around Mount Rushmore. Granite came crashing down the mountainside by the ton.

As the cutting got closer to the actual sculpting surface, workers had to be more careful. They used air-powered tools to remove the last few inches

A huge flag beside the head of George Washington commemorates its 1930 dedication.

of stone. Then more was broken off with hammers and wedges. Finally, the gleaming, solid rock underneath was exposed and ready for careful carving. The last, most precise cuts were made with hand chisels. Borglum observed from different angles and distances. He examined the work at various times of the day and night. He studied the way light and shadow played over the figures. Then he provided the final touches that gave the work life and feeling.

In this 1935 photograph, sculptors continue work on the face of George Washington.

One by one, the figures were completed. Washington was completed in 1930. Jefferson was unveiled in 1936. Lincoln followed in 1937, the 150th anniversary of the U.S. Constitution. Finally, Theodore Roosevelt was unveiled in 1939. It was nine years after the head of Washington had been completed, and fourteen years after Gutzon Borglum had first climbed Mount Rushmore.

President Franklin Delano Roosevelt attended the dedication of the Thomas Jefferson figure on August 30, 1936. His words that day make it clear that the memorial had a profound impact on him. "I had seen the photographs, I had seen

When the head of Thomas Jefferson was unveiled in 1936, work on the heads of Lincoln (covered by the flag) and Roosevelt was well under way.

Beneath the emerging face of Abraham Lincoln, the tons of granite that were blasted away from the mountain are clearly visible.

Although not yet completed, Roosevelt's head (surrounded by scaffolding) was unveiled on July 3, 1939.

the drawings, and I had talked with those who are responsible for this great work," he said. "And yet I had no conception, until about ten minutes ago, not only of its magnitude, but also of its permanent beauty and importance."

A final dedication of the monument was planned for 1941. But Gutzon Borglum would not survive that long. He died on a trip to Chicago, Illinois, that year, the result of a minor operation. The sculptor of Mount Rushmore was seventy-four. He didn't live long enough to see his sculpture completed. But he did live long enough to see his vision realized. He saw the images of America's great presidents emerge from the granite of the Black Hills of South Dakota.

Fittingly, Gutzon Borglum's son saw the project through to its close. After Gutzon Borglum's death, the Mount Rushmore workmen signed a petition asking that Lincoln Borglum be allowed to finish his father's work. Lincoln Borglum saw that the last details of the monument were completed.

In this 1941 photograph, Lincoln Borglum descends the mountainside to complete the finishing touches on the face of Abraham Lincoln.

There was plenty of work left for Lincoln Borglum to do. Details of the heads were still incomplete. The hair of each president had to be sculpted. And the rubble from years of blasting had to be cleared from the mountain. Lincoln Borglum did as much of this work as he could in the months following his father's death. But World War II (1939–45) was approaching. Once the United States was involved in that all-out effort, there would be precious little manpower or resources for the project on Mount Rushmore.

Work on the mountain shut down in October 1941 and never started again. In one sense, the sculpting work on Mount Rushmore was never completed. On the other hand, the figures on Mount Rushmore will remain for ages to come. They stand as an example of the sculptor's art, as a tribute to the will of the sculptor himself, and as a memorial to the presidents of a great nation.

On July 3, 1991, President George Bush spoke during the fiftieth anniversary celebration of Mount Rushmore.

GLOSSARY

appropriation – money set aside for a specific purpose

bunkhouse – simple building that serves as the sleeping quarters for a work crew

chisel – metal tool with a sharpened edge at one end used to chip, cut, or carve into a solid material

colossal

colossal – extremely large

daunting – frightening or discouraging

granite – very hard natural igneous rock formation

jackhammer – air-powered rock-drilling tool

Mesopotamians – ancient residents of Mesopotamia, a region in Southwest Asia

granite

monument – large structure or work of art erected in memory of a person or event

patrons – financial supporters of an artist or writer

republic – form of government in which the people elect representatives who manage the government

shrine – place or object with symbolic or sacred meaning and importance

weather-beaten – worn or damaged by exposure to the elements: rain, snow, wind, and sun

TIMELINE

1867 Gutzon Borglum born in Idaho

1901 Borglum's work purchased by
Metropolitan Museum of Art in New York

Borglum sculpts figure of Abraham **1909**
Lincoln, now in U.S. Capitol

1915 Borglum works on Stone Mountain
in Georgia

1924 Doane Robinson writes to Gutzon Borglum

1925

President Calvin Coolidge visits Black Hills **1927**

Figure of George Washington unveiled **1930**

Figure of Thomas Jefferson unveiled **1936**
Figure of Abraham Lincoln unveiled **1937**
Figure of Theodore Roosevelt unveiled **1939**

Gutzon Borglum dies; work continued **1941**
by Lincoln Borglum

Borglum
makes first
trip to Mount
Rushmore

INDEX *(Boldface page numbers indicate illustrations.)*

PHOTO CREDITS

Photographs ©: AP/Wide World Photos: 1, 13, 15, 18 bottom, 20, 21, 27 bottom, 28, 29, 30 bottom, 31 bottom left, 2 (Greg Latza); Bell Studio: 24; Charles D'Emery: 18 top, 23; Dave G. Houser: 5, 9; National Park Service: 19 (Julian Spotts), 17, 26; North Wind Picture Archives: 8, 12 bottom; Reverend Carl Loocke: 11; Rise Studio: 4, 10, 22, 31 top right, 31 bottom right; Root Resources: 3 (James Blank); Stock Montage, Inc.: 12 top, 12 (2nd from top), 12 (3rd from top), 25, 27 top, 30 top; Superstock, Inc.: cover, 7, 14.

ABOUT THE AUTHOR

Andrew Santella is a lifelong resident of Chicago, Illinois. He is a graduate of Chicago's Loyola University, where he studied American literature. He writes about history, sports, and popular culture for several magazines for young people. He is the author of several Children's Press titles, including *The Capitol, Jackie Robinson Breaks the Color Line, The Battle of the Alamo,* and *The Chisholm Trail* (Cornerstones of Freedom) and *Mo Vaughn* (Sports Stars).